Alex Karp

The Visionary Who Revolutionized
Technology and Changed the World

Clara Natasha

1

Alex Karp

Table of contents

Introduction: The Visionary Who Changed the World

- Discover how Alex Karp's early experiences shaped his vision for the future of technology, and how his leadership at Palantir has redefined the role of data in the modern world.

Chapter 1: Early Life and Education

- Discover Karp's formative years in Philadelphia, his academic journey, and how his philosophical background in social theory influenced his approach to technology and leadership.

Chapter 2: Founding Palantir Technologies

- Uncover the story of Palantir's creation, Karp's partnership with Peter Thiel, and how the company's mission to revolutionize data analytics was born from a desire to solve complex global challenges.

Chapter 3: Palantir's Growth and the Tech Revolution

- Learn about the challenges and triumphs Palantir experienced under Karp's leadership, and how the company grew to become a pivotal player in data security, analytics, and artificial intelligence.

Chapter 4: Revolutionizing Technology in Government and Beyond

- Discover Karp's work with government agencies and organizations around the world, and how Palantir's technology has been used to drive global change in fields ranging from national security to healthcare.

Chapter 5: Ethical Dilemmas and Controversies

- Find out the ethical challenges Karp has faced while navigating the use of powerful data analytics in sensitive areas, and how he has worked to address the concerns of privacy, surveillance, and responsibility.

Chapter 6: Karp's Leadership Philosophy and Vision

- Gain insight into Alex Karp's leadership style, his commitment to transparency, and his unique perspective on technology, innovation, and collaboration with government and private sectors.

Chapter 7: The Technological Landscape Under Karp's Influence

- Discover Karp's influence on the broader technological landscape, including his thoughts on the role of big tech in society, and how Palantir continues to impact industries ranging from defense to finance.

9. Chapter 8: A Look Toward the Future

- Reflect on Karp's vision for the future of technology, including advancements in artificial intelligence, machine learning, and the role of data in solving the world's most pressing issues.

Conclusion: A Legacy of Innovation and Impact

- Find out the enduring impact of Alex Karp's work on technology and society, and how his contributions continue to inspire innovation, shape industries, and influence future generations of tech leaders.

Appendices

A: Timeline of Key Milestones in Alex Karp's Career

B: Palantir's Major Projects and Achievements

C: Selected Writings and Speeches by Alex Karp

Introduction

The Visionary Who Changed the World

What does it take to revolutionize the way we see technology, data, and privacy in the 21st century? Can one individual truly shift the course of how societies interact with information and reshape the way organizations, governments, and institutions approach data? The answer, in this case, is Alex Karp.

As the co-founder and CEO of Palantir Technologies, Karp has carved a unique path in the tech industry, not through flashy marketing or viral products, but through a quiet, persistent vision that brings clarity to the often chaotic world of data. In this introduction, we will explore how Karp's early life, his academic journey, and his leadership at Palantir have combined to create a legacy that is changing the world in ways most people don't even realize.

Early Life: A Foundation in Thinking Differently

Alex Karp's life did not begin with a direct path to Silicon Valley. He wasn't born into a world of tech startups, and his academic interests were not initially focused on the realm of computers or engineering. Karp was born in 1967 in Philadelphia, to a family that valued education and intellectual rigor. His mother, a prominent physician, and his father, a well-regarded teacher, instilled in him a sense of curiosity, independence, and the importance of asking big questions.

Growing up, Karp struggled with dyslexia, a condition that can make reading and writing difficult. However, rather than discouraging him, this challenge shaped his way of thinking. Karp's experience with dyslexia fostered a mindset that pushed him to think outside the box, to seek understanding through different methods, and to confront problems in unconventional ways. This resilience would prove to be crucial as he embarked on his academic journey.

After high school, Karp attended the prestigious University of Chicago, where he initially studied history. While others may have followed more typical paths in engineering or technology, Karp's passion for social theory and philosophy led him to explore the intersections between technology, society, and governance. It was during these years that Karp's thinking began to mature in ways that would later shape his work with Palantir. His interest in the ethical implications of technology grew as he studied the work of renowned philosopher Jürgen Habermas, under whose mentorship Karp pursued a PhD in social theory at the Goethe University in Frankfurt.

Karp's academic background in social theory, paired with his deep curiosity about the intersection of technology and society, would lay the foundation for his future work. His studies taught him to question the ways in which technology could be used to shape social dynamics and political power. This intellectual framework would become critical as he helped create Palantir, a company that sits at the crossroads of data, security, and ethical questions.

The Birth of Palantir: A Vision to Change the World

In the early 2000s, Alex Karp co-founded Palantir Technologies with Peter Thiel and a team of other entrepreneurs. Palantir was born from a vision—a vision that recognized the growing importance of data in our world, but also understood the need for caution and responsibility in its use. The name "Palantir" comes from the "seeing-stones" in J.R.R. Tolkien's Lord of the Rings, which allowed users to view distant places and events. This metaphor perfectly encapsulated Karp's vision: to create tools that could allow users to "see" and understand complex data, empowering them to make better decisions while ensuring that such power wasn't abused.

Unlike many tech companies that focus on consumer-facing applications, Palantir set its sights on solving some of the most complex challenges in government and business. The company's flagship product, Palantir Foundry, was designed to help organizations make sense of large, complex datasets and draw actionable insights. Initially, the company's focus was on national security, helping intelligence agencies, defense organizations, and law enforcement sift through vast amounts of data to uncover critical patterns and prevent threats. However, Karp's vision extended far beyond these initial applications. He saw Palantir's potential to address societal challenges on a much larger scale.

One of the key differentiators of Palantir under Karp's leadership was its commitment to ensuring that its technology was used ethically. Palantir was built not just as a tool for analysis, but as a platform that would empower users to solve critical problems without compromising individual freedoms or rights. The company's technology was designed to give organizations the ability to uncover insights and drive decision-making without crossing the line into mass surveillance or exploitation of data. This was a delicate balancing act—one that Karp and his team were keenly aware of. From the very beginning, Palantir had to confront the ethical challenges posed by its powerful software.

Revolutionizing Data: Redefining the Role of Information in the Modern World

Karp's work with Palantir has not only changed the way data is understood and utilized but also helped redefine how information is viewed in the modern world. As the digital age has progressed, data has become one of the most valuable commodities. But Karp's vision was never just about making money off data—it was about empowering organizations and governments to use data in ways that could improve security, public health, and even the functioning of society itself.

Through Palantir's advanced data analytics, organizations have been able to tackle problems in ways that were previously impossible. For instance, Palantir has been used to help uncover patterns in global terrorism, track criminal networks, and even predict the spread of diseases. In addition, Palantir's software has been instrumental in the private sector, helping companies optimize supply chains, analyze market trends, and make data-driven decisions that have had a profound impact on industries ranging from finance to healthcare.

But the power of data also comes with immense responsibility, and Karp has been transparent about the ethical challenges that Palantir faces. He has consistently emphasized that technology should serve humanity, not the other way around. This philosophy has guided the company's approach to working with governments and businesses, and Karp has been at the forefront of conversations about how to balance innovation with accountability.

Karp has often spoken about the dangers of unregulated technology and the potential consequences of allowing powerful data analytics to fall into the wrong hands. He has been an advocate for greater oversight and transparency, not just for Palantir, but for the tech industry as a whole. His leadership has set a standard for how companies should approach the use of technology that has the potential to affect millions of lives.

A Visionary Leader: The Ethical Challenges and Triumphs

While many tech leaders are known for their bold moves and public personas, Alex Karp's leadership style has always been grounded in a strong sense of ethics and intellectual rigor. He is not the typical Silicon Valley CEO; rather than focusing solely on financial success, Karp has always prioritized the long-term impact of Palantir's work. This perspective has led him to make difficult decisions that have often set the company apart from other tech giants.

Karp's leadership has been marked by a willingness to confront uncomfortable truths and challenge the status quo. He has repeatedly expressed his concerns about the unchecked power of big tech companies and their ability to manipulate data for profit.

Karp's focus on maintaining Palantir's ethical standards, even in the face of significant pressure, has been one of the defining aspects of his leadership. His vision for the company has always been about creating technology that serves the greater good, even if that means making tough decisions or addressing uncomfortable issues.

Karp has also been a vocal advocate for greater transparency and accountability in the tech industry. He believes that the industry must move beyond the profit-driven mindset that has dominated Silicon Valley for decades. His views on this topic have earned him both admiration and criticism, but one thing is clear—he is not afraid to challenge the traditional narrative of what a tech company should be.

Legacy and Impact: The Visionary Who Continues to Shape the Future

As we look at Alex Karp's legacy, it becomes clear that his work is far from over. Karp's leadership at Palantir has already reshaped the way governments and businesses use data, but his influence reaches even further. His advocacy for ethical technology, transparency, and data-driven decision-making continues to inspire a new generation of leaders and entrepreneurs.

Karp's journey from a young academic with a passion for philosophy and social theory to the CEO of one of the most influential tech companies in the world is a testament to the power of vision, perseverance, and intellectual rigor. His work at Palantir has shown that technology can be a force for good, but only if it is used responsibly and with a deep understanding of its societal implications. The legacy of Alex Karp is one of innovation, leadership, and ethical stewardship—values that will continue to shape the world for years to come.

As the world continues to grapple with the implications of big data, artificial intelligence, and privacy concerns, Alex Karp's work will remain a beacon for how technology can be used to benefit humanity. His legacy is one that has already transformed industries and will continue to influence the way technology impacts our lives in profound ways.

Chapter 1

Early Life and Education

The Seeds of a Visionary

In the heart of Philadelphia, a city known for its rich history and intellectual vibrance, a future tech visionary was being shaped. Alex Karp, born in 1967, came into the world not with the traditional hallmarks of a Silicon Valley prodigy—no early coding feats, no childhood company launches. Instead, his story begins in a place where intellectual curiosity, resilience, and deep thought would become the foundation for a lifetime of revolutionizing technology. What makes Alex Karp's journey so unique is not simply his academic achievements or his rise as a technology leader, but the ways in which his early life and education shaped his perspective on data, society, and ethics—perspectives that would later guide Palantir Technologies into a global powerhouse.

Karp's early life was marked by both privilege and struggle. Growing up in a household that valued education and intellectual rigor, Karp's parents were instrumental in shaping his worldview. His mother, a physician, and his father, a teacher, instilled in him a deep appreciation for knowledge, and, perhaps more importantly, an understanding of how societal structures and human behavior intersect. However, despite the benefits of a solid academic upbringing, Karp was not immune to challenges. Like many innovators, he had to confront personal obstacles that would ultimately mold his approach to leadership and technology.

Early Years: A Foundation in Resilience

Alex Karp's academic journey wasn't the smoothest, but it laid the groundwork for his future success. Diagnosed with dyslexia at a young age, Karp's struggles with reading and writing were immediate challenges. But rather than allowing these obstacles to define him, he developed the resilience to push through them. For many, dyslexia is a source of frustration or even shame, but Karp turned it into a unique tool for navigating the world. Rather than viewing his learning disability as a weakness, Karp began to approach problems from different angles, finding creative ways to solve them. This mindset would later influence his leadership style—one that prizes innovative thinking and out-of-the-box solutions.

Karp's educational environment—one where intellectual rigor was valued and where questions were encouraged—helped him to reframe the way he approached problems. It was here, during these early years, that he first learned the importance of asking "Why?" rather than simply accepting conventional answers. This intellectual curiosity would later become a hallmark of his leadership at Palantir.

Despite his academic struggles, Karp excelled in other areas. His passion for history and social theory drove him to pursue a path in academia. What sets Karp apart from many tech visionaries is his deep interest in philosophy and social thought. Unlike the stereotypical tech mogul focused solely on programming or engineering, Karp was drawn to the abstract realms of social theory, ethics, and how technological advancements impact human societies.

Academic Journey: The Path to Philosophy

Alex Karp's time at the University of Chicago would mark a turning point in his intellectual development. The university, renowned for its rigorous academic standards, was where Karp's interest in philosophy and social theory truly took root. He studied under some of the most brilliant minds in the field, but it was the ideas of German philosopher Jürgen Habermas that would profoundly shape Karp's views on technology, politics, and society.

Habermas's work, particularly his ideas on communication theory and the role of rational discourse in society, deeply resonated with Karp. The notion that society could function more effectively if its members engaged in thoughtful, ethical discussions was an idea that stuck with him. Karp found himself captivated by the complexities of human behavior in the context of systems and structures. These ideas would later inform his approach to Palantir, as Karp sought to create technology that could empower organizations to think critically and make informed decisions, while also considering the ethical consequences of using that data.

At the University of Chicago, Karp wasn't just focused on acquiring a degree—he was immersing himself in a deep intellectual journey that would ultimately set him apart in the tech world. It was here that Karp developed an analytical mindset that emphasized understanding the broader social context of technology. While many of his peers were focused on building the next big software or application, Karp was concerned with the larger implications of those technologies on the world.

Social Theory and Leadership: A Unique Approach

Karp's philosophical background in social theory didn't just shape his academic perspective; it directly influenced how he approached leadership at Palantir. Karp's understanding of societal structures and human interactions made him acutely aware of the potential for technology to disrupt those systems, both positively and negatively. This was a critical insight for him as he began to build Palantir. Where other tech companies were rushing to innovate without fully considering the long-term impact of their technologies, Karp was already thinking about the ethical dilemmas that would arise as data began to play an increasingly larger role in our lives.

Karp's ability to blend technical prowess with philosophical depth set him apart from other tech founders. While many tech leaders have backgrounds in engineering or mathematics, Karp's training in social theory allowed him to view data not just as numbers but as a tool that could fundamentally reshape human behavior and societal outcomes. This made him not just a visionary in the world of technology, but a leader who approached technological innovation with a sense of responsibility.

At Palantir, Karp's philosophical framework played an essential role in the company's development. Unlike many tech companies that were solely focused on profitability or growth, Karp insisted that Palantir's mission be guided by a deeper understanding of the social consequences of its technology. This vision is reflected in Palantir's core mission: to help organizations make sense of large, complex datasets while also being mindful of the ethical and societal implications of doing so.

Karp's Influences: Intellectual and Philosophical Underpinnings

While Jürgen Habermas was one of Karp's most significant intellectual influences, other thinkers also shaped his worldview. Karp has often pointed to his exposure to critical theory, particularly from the Frankfurt School, as an important part of his intellectual development. This group of scholars, who examined the ways in which culture, politics, and economics intersect, gave Karp the tools to think about technology as more than just a tool for innovation—it became a lens through which he could understand the power dynamics at play in society.

This intellectual background was crucial as Karp entered the world of Silicon Valley, where technology companies were rapidly changing the world. But Karp didn't approach this change with blind optimism. He was critical of the unchecked power that large tech companies could wield, and he remained focused on the need for ethical considerations in technological development.

Karp's philosophical training also influenced his views on the role of the individual in a technological society. His academic interests led him to question the traditional top-down approach that many organizations adopt. Instead, he advocated for a more collaborative and open approach to data, one that emphasized transparency and ethical decision-making.

A Philosopher in the Tech World

What makes Karp's journey even more remarkable is the intersection of philosophy and technology in his life. The tech world, with its fast-paced innovation and drive for profit, often seems disconnected from the ethical considerations that philosophers like Habermas stress. However, Karp proved that these two worlds don't have to be separate. By applying his understanding of social theory to the realm of technology, he created a company that didn't just focus on profit but on how technology could be used to solve real-world problems while considering its impact on society.

This unique perspective has made Karp a rare figure in the tech world—one who combines intellectual rigor with the ability to build a successful company that impacts the world. His leadership style is reflective of his academic background—thoughtful, introspective, and ethical. He has consistently emphasized the need for technology to be used responsibly, with consideration for both its positive and negative effects on society.

Conclusion: The Shaping of a Visionary Leader

Alex Karp's early life and education laid the foundation for the visionary leadership that would define his career. From his struggles with dyslexia to his academic achievements in social theory, Karp developed a unique perspective that would later inform his leadership at Palantir. His philosophical background, which taught him to ask critical questions and consider the broader implications of technology, set him apart from his peers in the tech industry.

As Karp's journey progressed from a student of social theory to a tech entrepreneur, his commitment to ethical innovation became a central theme. Palantir was not just about technology—it was about creating solutions that had the potential to improve society while being mindful of the consequences of that technology. In many ways, Karp's background in philosophy and social theory was the key to his success, as it provided him with the intellectual tools to navigate the ethical and societal challenges of the modern world.

This chapter offers a glimpse into the formative years that shaped Alex Karp into the visionary leader he is today. His early life, education, and philosophical influences have given him a unique outlook on technology and leadership, one that continues to drive Palantir's mission to this day. And as we move forward in this book, we will see how Karp's intellectual foundation has influenced not only his company's success but also his broader impact on the world of technology, data, and society.

Chapter 2

Founding Palantir Technologies

The story of Palantir Technologies is more than just a tale of a tech company's rise—it is the story of how one visionary, armed with a philosophical background and a burning desire to make an impact, sought to solve some of the most complex global challenges of the 21st century. For Alex Karp, Palantir's creation wasn't about chasing after a fast profit or following the well-worn path of Silicon Valley success. Instead, it was born out of an intellectual drive to address some of the world's most pressing issues—issues like terrorism, financial crimes, and data security—using cutting-edge technology to give governments, businesses, and organizations the tools to make better decisions.

In the early 2000s, Karp was at a crossroads in his career. A social theorist by training, he was acutely aware of the rapidly changing landscape of technology, particularly in the areas of data and intelligence. Karp, along with a group of like-minded visionaries, saw that data was becoming one of the most valuable assets in the modern world. But they also understood that data—when handled poorly—could easily be misused or misinterpreted, leading to disastrous consequences. This was where Palantir came in.

The Genesis of Palantir: The Birth of a Tech Visionary

The origins of Palantir can be traced back to Alex Karp's partnership with Peter Thiel, co-founder of PayPal and a well-known figure in the world of technology and venture capital. In 2003, Peter Thiel was already a successful entrepreneur, and he had begun to identify the growing power of data as a key factor in future technological and economic development. But Thiel, much like Karp, recognized that the potential of data could not be fully realized without addressing the deep ethical and societal challenges it posed.

It was during this time that Karp and Thiel crossed paths. Karp's background in social theory and philosophy made him a unique partner for Thiel, who was more focused on business and innovation. Where many others in the tech industry were eager to exploit data for commercial gain, Karp saw the potential dangers of such unregulated power. The two men were aligned in their vision: data, when harnessed responsibly, could be used to solve major global challenges, but it also required a strong ethical foundation.

Together, they founded Palantir in 2004, a company that would go on to revolutionize the way governments and private organizations use data. The name "Palantir" was inspired by J.R.R. Tolkien's Lord of the Rings—specifically, the "Palantíri," which were seeing stones that allowed their users to view distant places. In the context of the company, the name symbolized the ability to gain clear insight from vast, complex datasets, enabling those with the right tools to "see" and understand hidden patterns and critical information.

While the concept of data analytics wasn't new, Palantir's approach to solving these challenges was groundbreaking. The company's mission was not just about creating another software tool for data analysis—it was about providing organizations with the power to unlock the full potential of their data while respecting privacy and security. Karp and Thiel's shared belief in the ethical use of technology would become the foundation of Palantir's culture.

The Vision: Revolutionizing Data Analytics

From its inception, Palantir set out to address some of the most complex and pressing global challenges. The company's primary focus was on government applications, particularly in the areas of national security and defense. At the time, U.S. intelligence agencies were grappling with the overwhelming task of analyzing massive amounts of data to identify threats and patterns related to terrorism. The problem wasn't just about collecting data—it was about making sense of it.

Karp and Thiel realized that traditional methods of data analysis were ill-equipped to handle the complexity and scale of modern intelligence operations. Existing systems were slow, inefficient, and often resulted in key information being overlooked or buried under an avalanche of irrelevant data. Palantir's vision was to create a platform that could sift through massive datasets and deliver actionable insights to intelligence officers in real time.

To make this vision a reality, Palantir introduced its flagship product, Palantir

Foundry, a data analytics platform designed to enable organizations to integrate, visualize, and analyze large-scale data. The core strength of Foundry was its ability to process both structured and unstructured data, allowing users to uncover hidden patterns and make data-driven decisions that had real-world consequences.

The company's approach was revolutionary for several reasons. First, Palantir emphasized a user-friendly interface that enabled analysts and decision-makers to interact with data in ways that were previously only possible for highly specialized professionals. This democratization of data analysis meant that anyone in an organization, regardless of their technical expertise, could engage with complex datasets and derive meaningful insights.

Second, Palantir's focus on security and privacy was integral to its mission. Karp, with his deep understanding of social theory and ethics, understood that the power of data came with significant risks. He was committed to ensuring that Palantir's software was used responsibly. This focus on security and ethical use of technology became a central tenet of Palantir's business model, distinguishing it from many of its competitors in the tech space.

The Early Challenges: Building a Culture of Innovation

In its early days, Palantir faced a variety of challenges. The tech world was skeptical of the company's approach, which emphasized the ethical use of data rather than maximizing profits through mass surveillance or exploitation. While companies like Google and Facebook were using data to drive advertising revenue, Palantir's model was different—it was about providing tools for good, tools that could be used to protect individuals and societies from harm.

One of Palantir's early breakthroughs came when it was able to successfully deploy its technology in counterterrorism efforts. After the September 11 attacks, U.S. intelligence agencies were under immense pressure to find ways to prevent future terrorist acts. Palantir's software proved to be an invaluable tool in this effort, helping analysts sift through vast amounts of data to uncover hidden terrorist networks and thwart potential attacks.

However, this success did not come without controversy. Palantir's close ties to government agencies, particularly in the areas of surveillance and national security, led to concerns about privacy and civil liberties. Karp, though, remained steadfast in his belief that Palantir's technology could be used responsibly to protect individuals and secure societies. He was determined to build a company that not only helped solve complex problems but did so with a clear commitment to ethical standards.

Palantir's early years were marked by constant innovation, as the company continued to refine its technology and expand its offerings. As the company grew, so did its customer base. By the mid-2000s, Palantir had attracted major clients in both government and the private sector, including law enforcement agencies, financial institutions, and healthcare organizations.

Palantir's Expanding Reach: Transforming Multiple Industries

As Palantir's technology matured, its applications expanded beyond national security. The company's data analytics platforms began to gain traction in other industries, including finance, healthcare, and energy. In each of these sectors, Palantir's software allowed organizations to analyze large datasets, uncover trends, and make more informed decisions.

For example, in the healthcare industry, Palantir's technology was used to identify patterns in patient data that could help improve medical outcomes and streamline operations. In the financial sector, Palantir's software was used to combat fraud and improve risk management. These applications showcased the versatility of Palantir's technology and its potential to solve a wide range of complex problems across various industries.

However, it was Palantir's continued commitment to data privacy and security that distinguished it from many other tech companies. As data-driven decision-making became more prevalent, the risks associated with mishandling sensitive information grew exponentially. Palantir's focus on responsible data usage and its commitment to protecting the privacy of individuals remained a core part of its business model, even as the company expanded into new markets.

The Legacy: A Vision Realized

Today, Palantir Technologies stands as one of the most influential companies in the world of data analytics. Its products are used by government agencies, Fortune 500 companies, and nonprofits around the world to solve complex problems and make data-driven decisions. Palantir has grown far beyond its early work in national security to become a global leader in data analytics, with applications in industries ranging from healthcare to finance, manufacturing, and beyond.

Through Karp's leadership, Palantir has remained true to its founding vision of using technology for good, empowering organizations to tackle the world's most challenging problems. Karp's intellectual foundation in social theory, coupled with his deep commitment to the ethical use of technology, has shaped Palantir into a company that seeks to transform industries while respecting the privacy and rights of individuals.

As Palantir continues to grow and innovate, its commitment to solving complex global challenges remains unwavering. The company's ability to turn data into actionable insights is helping shape the future of industries across the world, and its ethical approach to technology is setting a new standard for how data should be handled in the modern age.

Conclusion: Palantir's Ongoing Impact

The founding of Palantir Technologies is a story of vision, innovation, and ethical commitment. What began as a small startup focused on solving national security challenges has since become a global leader in data analytics, transforming industries and helping organizations solve some of the world's most pressing problems. The company's success is a testament to the power of using technology responsibly, and Karp's vision for Palantir continues to shape the way we think about data and its potential to drive change.

As we look ahead, it's clear that the story of Palantir is far from over. With Karp's continued leadership, the company is poised to tackle even more complex global challenges and make an even greater impact on the world. The creation of Palantir has changed the way we understand data, and its legacy will continue to influence the future of technology and society for years to come.

Chapter 3

Palantir's Growth and the Tech Revolution

The world of technology has always been one of rapid change, where ideas are born, evolve, and either soar to success or falter in obscurity. In the early days of the tech revolution, many companies tried to harness the power of data. However, very few companies were able to address the scale, complexity, and societal implications of data in the way that Palantir Technologies, under the leadership of Alex Karp, has done. This chapter focuses on Palantir's remarkable growth, the challenges it faced, and the way it became a pivotal player in the fields of data security, analytics, and artificial intelligence (AI).

The Initial Struggles and Strategic Beginnings

Palantir's journey began at a time when the tech industry was dominated by giants who had already established themselves— companies like Microsoft, Google, and Facebook. These companies were leading the charge in consumer-facing technologies, like search engines, social media platforms, and operating systems. In contrast, Palantir's goal was more specialized: it aimed to harness data analytics for solving complex, high-stakes problems in fields like national security and government intelligence.

From the very beginning, Palantir faced an uphill battle. While the potential of data was becoming clear, its ethical and practical applications remained in question. Many companies in the tech industry were hesitant to engage with government entities, fearing the political and societal backlash that could arise from working with intelligence agencies or law enforcement. Palantir, however, was determined to carve out a unique space for itself—one that was built on solving real-world problems, particularly in the realms of security and governance.

The company's first major challenge was establishing its legitimacy and credibility, particularly given the sensitive nature of the work it was undertaking. While Palantir's data analytics software had immense potential, convincing clients in the government and intelligence sectors to trust a new, unproven company was no easy task. Many of Palantir's early projects were met with skepticism. How could a tech startup with limited resources and no track record convince the U.S. government, or any large institution, that it had the tools necessary to tackle the data-driven challenges of the modern world?

Under Karp's leadership, Palantir focused on one key idea: building a tool that could integrate diverse datasets, helping agencies and organizations work more efficiently and make better decisions. Rather than pushing for broad adoption of its technology, Palantir chose to work on a smaller scale, ensuring that its products were built to meet the real needs of its clients. This approach allowed the company to establish trust, build successful relationships, and prove the value of its technology through actual performance.

The Turning Point: Overcoming Early Doubts

One of the pivotal moments in Palantir's growth came when it secured its first major contract with the U.S. government. Palantir's software was used to help track and prevent terrorist activities, a challenge that the intelligence community was struggling to address in the aftermath of the September 11 attacks. Palantir's technology provided a powerful, user-friendly way to analyze vast amounts of data from a variety of sources. It allowed intelligence agencies to connect the dots in ways that traditional methods could not, leading to better decision-making and more efficient operations.

This breakthrough was a turning point for Palantir. Once the company's technology was put to the test in such a high-stakes environment, it quickly became clear that the company had developed something truly revolutionary. Palantir's software wasn't just another database or analytics tool—it was an advanced platform that could bring together disparate datasets, uncover hidden patterns, and generate actionable intelligence in real-time.

The successful implementation of Palantir's software in the intelligence community not only validated the company's business model, but it also positioned Palantir as a crucial player in the growing field of data analytics. The company's reputation grew rapidly, and soon Palantir was attracting attention from sectors beyond national security—industries like finance, healthcare, and even retail.

But the journey was far from over. While Palantir had achieved success in its initial government contracts, the company faced numerous challenges as it expanded. One of the primary hurdles was ensuring that the technology could be scaled up without compromising its ability to deliver accurate, actionable insights. As Palantir grew, so did its client base and the complexity of the problems it was being asked to solve. At each step, the company had to balance innovation with reliability, always pushing the boundaries of what was possible while maintaining a focus on ethical data use.

Palantir's Expansion: Beyond Government to Private Industry

As Palantir's technology proved itself in the government and defense sectors, the company began to look toward expanding its reach into the private sector. Many companies had begun to see the value of data-driven decision-making, but few had the tools or the expertise to truly harness the potential of their data. Palantir recognized this gap and set out to provide the same cutting-edge tools to organizations outside of government agencies.

The shift to the private sector wasn't easy, however. It meant adapting Palantir's technology to new industries with different needs and demands. For example, in the financial sector, Palantir's software was used to help banks detect fraudulent activities and manage risk. In healthcare, it allowed organizations to analyze patient data more effectively, helping to identify trends that could lead to better patient outcomes.

Perhaps one of the most significant challenges Palantir faced during this time was convincing potential clients that its software wasn't just a tool for large-scale government operations—it could also be useful for smaller, more agile businesses. Many organizations were hesitant to adopt Palantir's technology, seeing it as a tool designed exclusively for national security, rather than a product that could be customized for a variety of industries.

To overcome this challenge, Palantir worked closely with clients to develop tailored solutions that met their specific needs. This collaborative approach allowed the company to enter new markets successfully and broaden its client base. By the time Palantir expanded into industries like finance, healthcare, and manufacturing, it had established itself as a reliable partner capable of solving complex data challenges across different sectors.

Artificial Intelligence and the Future of Data Analytics

A key factor that set Palantir apart from other tech companies was its commitment to advancing artificial intelligence (AI) and machine learning. While many tech companies were content to rely on traditional methods of data analysis, Palantir recognized that the future of data analytics lay in AI and machine learning, which could process and analyze vast amounts of data far more efficiently than any human could.

Under Karp's leadership, Palantir began to integrate AI into its products, allowing organizations to not only analyze historical data but also predict future trends based on that data. The company's AI-powered tools made it possible to uncover patterns and connections that would have been impossible to detect using traditional methods. This integration of AI not only enhanced Palantir's offerings but also solidified the company's reputation as an innovative leader in the field of data analytics.

Palantir's AI-driven platforms are now used by some of the world's most advanced organizations, helping them to make data-driven decisions in real time. Whether it's predicting financial market trends, identifying public health risks, or optimizing supply chains, Palantir's technology is helping to shape the future of data analytics and artificial intelligence.

Challenges of Growth: Maintaining Ethics and Security

As Palantir grew, so did the pressure to maintain the ethical standards that had been set during the company's early days. Palantir's deep involvement with government agencies and sensitive data meant that it was constantly scrutinized for its handling of privacy and security. While many tech companies were focused on maximizing profits, Palantir remained committed to its mission of providing tools that could solve important societal problems while protecting individual rights.

The ethical challenges were particularly pronounced as the company expanded into the private sector. Palantir had to navigate complex questions around privacy, data security, and consent. Karp, whose philosophical background made him uniquely suited to addressing these issues, continued to steer the company toward responsible data usage. He emphasized that Palantir's technology should never be used to infringe on individual rights, and that its clients needed to ensure that their use of the company's software aligned with ethical standards.

Despite these challenges, Palantir's commitment to ethical data use helped the company maintain its integrity and differentiate itself from other tech giants. While Palantir's competitors focused on profit-driven models, Karp's leadership ensured that the company remained focused on its core mission: using data to improve decision-making and solve complex global problems while safeguarding privacy and security.

Conclusion: Palantir's Legacy and the Future of Data Analytics

Palantir's growth is a testament to the power of innovation, resilience, and ethical leadership. From its humble beginnings as a small startup focused on solving national security challenges, the company has grown into one of the most influential players in the world of data analytics, artificial intelligence, and data security.

Under Alex Karp's leadership, Palantir has not only revolutionized the way organizations use data but also set a new standard for how technology can be used responsibly. The company's focus on ethics, security, and social good has allowed it to navigate the challenges of rapid growth while staying true to its founding principles.

As we look to the future, Palantir's role in the world of data analytics and AI is poised to become even more significant. With the increasing reliance on data-driven decision-making, Palantir is well-positioned to continue solving some of the world's most complex problems, from national security to healthcare to environmental sustainability.

The company's journey, under Karp's visionary leadership, has shown that data is more than just information—it is a powerful tool for change, and it can be used for good, when guided by ethical principles and a vision for the future.

Chapter 4

Revolutionizing Technology in Government and Beyond

In the world of technology, there are moments when a new idea, a new tool, or a new method can transform entire industries. For Alex Karp, the co-founder and CEO of Palantir Technologies, the vision for Palantir was never just about creating another tech product—it was about changing how organizations, governments, and people interact with data in ways that could impact global security, public health, and societal advancement. Palantir's journey from a small Silicon Valley startup to a technology giant is built on the company's core mission to drive global change by revolutionizing how data is analyzed, interpreted, and utilized.

This chapter delves into Karp's work with government agencies, international organizations, and private entities around the world. It explores how Palantir's technology has been applied across various sectors—particularly in national security, healthcare, and more—and examines the ways in which Karp's leadership has allowed the company to play a key role in addressing some of the world's most urgent challenges.

Palantir's Technology and National Security

From the very beginning, Palantir's mission was closely tied to national security. The company was founded in the aftermath of the 9/11 terrorist attacks, a pivotal moment in history that created an urgent need for advanced data analytics in intelligence and security operations. The attacks highlighted the inability of traditional intelligence agencies to effectively analyze vast amounts of data and identify terrorist cells or potential threats.

Karp and his co-founders recognized the need for a tool that could handle and make sense of large datasets—data that could range from phone records and email communication to satellite imagery and financial transactions. Palantir's flagship product, Palantir Foundry, was designed with this purpose in mind: to provide governments with a powerful, scalable platform for integrating and analyzing data, uncovering patterns, and making better decisions. Unlike traditional intelligence software, Palantir offered a user-friendly interface that allowed analysts to engage with data and extract meaningful insights without the need for specialized technical skills.

One of Palantir's earliest breakthroughs came with its adoption by U.S. government agencies. The company's software was deployed to the U.S. Department of Defense, the Central Intelligence Agency (CIA), and other intelligence agencies to help uncover terrorist networks and prevent attacks. Palantir's ability to aggregate and analyze data from various sources allowed intelligence officers to connect the dots in ways that traditional systems could not.

But Palantir's success was not just about providing the technology—it was about changing the way intelligence agencies approached their work. Karp emphasized that Palantir's software was not a "black box" solution but a platform that encouraged collaboration between analysts. Palantir's interface allowed users to add context to the data, creating a more interactive and dynamic process that went beyond simply storing and reporting information. As a result, Palantir helped transform how governments approached counterterrorism and national security, making it possible to prevent terrorist attacks by analyzing data in real time and uncovering actionable intelligence.

Global Expansion: Palantir's Reach Beyond the U.S. Government

While Palantir's technology was initially developed to address U.S. national security needs, its applications quickly expanded to governments and organizations worldwide. The company's ability to analyze complex data made it an invaluable tool for governments grappling with a wide array of challenges. Palantir's software was used to track and combat drug cartels in South America, help authorities respond to humanitarian crises in Africa, and even assist European governments in addressing cybersecurity threats.

One of the key factors in Palantir's global expansion was the company's commitment to understanding the unique needs of each client. Rather than adopting a one-size-fits-all approach, Palantir worked closely with its government and organizational clients to tailor its software solutions to their specific requirements. This adaptability and attention to local context made Palantir's technology indispensable in solving a diverse range of problems across the world.

For example, in 2015, Palantir began working with the United Kingdom's National Health Service (NHS) to help improve patient care and manage resources more effectively. By integrating data from hospitals, clinics, and other healthcare facilities, Palantir's software provided a more holistic view of the healthcare system, allowing authorities to identify trends, allocate resources efficiently, and address patient needs with greater accuracy. In a world where healthcare data is often siloed and fragmented, Palantir's ability to bring together disparate datasets has proven to be a game-changer.

Palantir also played a critical role in the fight against the COVID-19 pandemic. When the pandemic first began to spread, governments around the world were faced with the challenge of making rapid decisions based on limited and often incomplete data. Palantir's software enabled organizations to analyze vast amounts of health data, track the spread of the virus, and predict how healthcare systems would be impacted. Palantir's technology also supported vaccine distribution efforts, helping governments to monitor the effectiveness of vaccines and track their deployment to ensure that resources were allocated where they were needed most.

The Role of Palantir in Healthcare

Healthcare is one of the most data-intensive sectors in the world, with vast amounts of patient information, clinical data, and research findings that need to be analyzed in order to improve care and outcomes. Palantir recognized early on that healthcare, much like national security, could benefit from advanced data analytics. However, the challenge was not only about analyzing medical data—it was about integrating that data across systems, organizations, and even countries.

In partnership with healthcare providers, Palantir has worked to create solutions that bridge the gaps in healthcare data systems. One of the company's notable projects involved working with hospitals and healthcare institutions to track patient health records and monitor hospital performance. By integrating data across multiple hospitals and clinics, Palantir enabled healthcare organizations to identify patterns in patient outcomes, optimize treatment plans, and ensure that patients received the care they needed in a timely manner.

One of the key applications of Palantir's technology in healthcare is its ability to improve predictive analytics. By analyzing historical data, Palantir's software can help predict patient outcomes, such as the likelihood of readmission or the success rate of a particular treatment. This predictive capability allows healthcare professionals to take a more proactive approach to patient care, reducing the risk of complications and improving overall health outcomes.

Additionally, Palantir has been instrumental in helping public health organizations respond to global health crises, including disease outbreaks and epidemics. The company's software has enabled organizations like the World Health Organization (WHO) and the Centers for Disease Control and Prevention (CDC) to track the spread of infectious diseases and predict how they might evolve. Palantir's ability to provide real-time insights has been critical in managing the COVID-19 pandemic and ensuring that resources were allocated to areas experiencing the greatest need.

Palantir in Business: The Private Sector Revolution

While Palantir initially focused on government clients, its technology quickly proved invaluable to the private sector as well. Companies in industries such as finance, energy, and retail began to recognize the power of Palantir's software in managing and analyzing large datasets. In fact, Palantir's success in the private sector has been instrumental in cementing its reputation as a leader in data analytics.

In the finance industry, Palantir's technology has been used to detect fraud, manage risk, and optimize trading strategies. By analyzing financial transactions and uncovering patterns in customer behavior, Palantir helps companies identify potentially fraudulent activities before they escalate. The company's platform has also been used to optimize supply chains, improve inventory management, and predict market trends, giving businesses a competitive edge in an increasingly data-driven world.

In the energy sector, Palantir's software has been used to optimize operations and improve resource management. By analyzing data from sensors and equipment, Palantir helps energy companies identify inefficiencies, reduce downtime, and ensure that resources are allocated in the most cost-effective way. This ability to optimize operations is particularly valuable in industries where margins are thin, and every ounce of efficiency counts.

The Ethical Challenges and Social Responsibility

Despite Palantir's successes, the company has faced its fair share of criticism. Many have raised concerns about the potential misuse of Palantir's technology, particularly when it comes to issues of privacy and surveillance. As a company that works with sensitive data, Palantir has had to navigate the complex ethical questions surrounding its use of technology.

Under Karp's leadership, the company has consistently emphasized the importance of using its technology responsibly. Karp has been vocal about the ethical challenges of working with data and has repeatedly stressed that Palantir is committed to ensuring that its software is used for the benefit of society. This commitment to ethical standards has been one of the defining features of the company, setting it apart from other tech giants that prioritize profit over privacy and security.

Palantir's work in government and healthcare has demonstrated the company's commitment to making a positive impact on society. By addressing some of the world's most complex challenges—whether it's preventing terrorism, improving healthcare outcomes, or addressing environmental issues—Palantir has proven that data, when used responsibly, can drive meaningful change.

Conclusion: A Global Change-Maker

From its work with governments to its impact on industries like healthcare, finance, and energy, Palantir Technologies has firmly established itself as a leader in the field of data analytics. Under the visionary leadership of Alex Karp, Palantir's technology has not only revolutionized how organizations use data but has also driven global change by addressing some of the most critical issues of our time.

As we continue to face complex challenges in an increasingly data-driven world, Palantir's role as a tech innovator remains more relevant than ever. Whether in government, healthcare, or business, Palantir's technology is helping organizations make smarter decisions, protect individuals, and solve the world's most pressing problems.

Alex Karp

Chapter 5

Ethical Dilemmas and Controversies

In an era where data is considered the new oil, the power of technology to shape societies, economies, and personal lives is undeniable. However, with this power comes an inherent responsibility, especially when it comes to how data is collected, stored, and used. Few individuals understand this better than Alex Karp, the CEO of Palantir Technologies. Under his leadership, Palantir has become one of the world's leading companies in data analytics, but this success has not come without its share of ethical challenges and controversies. In this chapter, we examine the difficult ethical dilemmas Karp has faced as Palantir has navigated the complex landscape of data privacy, surveillance, and the responsibility that comes with wielding such powerful technology.

Palantir's Ethical Mission: A Double-Edged Sword

Palantir Technologies was founded with a clear mission: to harness the power of data to solve critical, real-world problems—particularly in national security, healthcare, and other industries where large amounts of complex data need to be analyzed. From its inception, the company's technology has been a game-changer, providing governments, intelligence agencies, and private businesses with powerful tools for analyzing data and making informed decisions.

Yet, while Palantir's products have been instrumental in solving complex problems, they have also raised serious concerns about privacy and the ethical use of data. The company's close relationships with government agencies, particularly in the intelligence and defense sectors, have brought Palantir to the forefront of debates surrounding surveillance, civil liberties, and the role of technology in modern governance.

At the heart of Palantir's ethical challenges is the tension between the potential benefits of using data for national security, law enforcement, and public health and the risks associated with infringing upon individual privacy and civil rights. The company has long been accused of enabling surveillance practices that could compromise the freedoms it aims to protect. Karp, however, has always maintained that Palantir's technology is not intended for mass surveillance but is meant to help organizations make data-driven decisions to tackle major societal challenges.

While Karp has been unwavering in his defense of Palantir's mission, he has also acknowledged the ethical responsibilities that come with handling such powerful technology. For Karp, the ethical use of

Palantir's data analytics tools has been a central theme of his leadership. He recognizes that the line between using data for good and exploiting it for nefarious purposes is thin, and he is keenly aware of the societal implications of his company's work.

The National Security Debate: Privacy vs. Protection

Palantir's earliest and most high-profile work was with U.S. government agencies, particularly in the wake of the September 11 attacks. The company's technology was seen as a critical tool for preventing future terrorist attacks by enabling intelligence agencies to analyze vast amounts of data from disparate sources. Palantir's software was used to track and analyze phone calls, financial transactions, communications, and other data in ways that were previously impossible.

While Palantir's role in helping to prevent terrorist attacks is often hailed as a success, it has also raised concerns about privacy and the potential abuse of power. Critics argue that the same tools used to track terrorists could be turned against the public, potentially enabling mass surveillance and infringing on individuals' privacy rights. The line between national security and personal freedoms is a delicate one, and many worry that Palantir's technology could tip the balance in favor of surveillance at the expense of civil liberties.

Karp has faced these concerns head-on. On multiple occasions, he has defended Palantir's work, insisting that the company is committed to ensuring that its software is used for good and in accordance with the law. He has emphasized that Palantir's technology is not designed for blanket surveillance but for the specific purpose of enabling organizations to find critical patterns in data that could help save lives and protect national security. Karp has argued that the benefits of using Palantir's software to fight terrorism, cybercrime, and other threats far outweigh the potential risks of privacy violations.

Despite Karp's defense, the ethical debate surrounding Palantir's role in national security continues to be a source of controversy. Critics argue that the company's work with intelligence agencies could contribute to a surveillance state, where citizens are constantly monitored and their personal data is collected without their knowledge or consent. This debate is ongoing, and Karp's stance on these issues has been crucial in shaping Palantir's public image.

The Healthcare Conundrum: Balancing Innovation with Privacy

Palantir's work in the healthcare industry has been equally transformative, providing hospitals, research institutions, and public health organizations with the tools they need to analyze large sets of medical data. By integrating data from various sources—such as patient records, clinical trials, and even wearable devices—Palantir has helped organizations improve patient outcomes, optimize resources, and streamline operations.

But healthcare is an industry where privacy concerns are especially heightened. The data being analyzed is often sensitive, and any breach of patient confidentiality can have dire consequences. The ethical challenges in healthcare are compounded by the increasing use of artificial intelligence (AI) and machine learning, which Palantir has incorporated into its software. While AI has the potential to revolutionize healthcare, it also raises questions about data ownership, consent, and security.

Palantir has made strides in addressing these concerns by emphasizing its commitment to data privacy and security. The company has worked closely with healthcare organizations to ensure that its technology complies with regulations like the Health Insurance Portability and Accountability Act (HIPAA), which mandates the protection of patient information. However, critics argue that the very nature of Palantir's work—integrating data from multiple sources—could lead to unintended privacy violations, especially if the data is accessed or used improperly.

Karp's response to these concerns has been one of transparency. He has repeatedly emphasized that Palantir's technology is not a "black box" but an open and collaborative platform that allows organizations to make informed decisions about how data is used. Karp has also defended the idea that, while privacy is a significant concern, the potential benefits of improving healthcare outcomes and saving lives outweigh the risks of data misuse.

The challenge for Karp and Palantir, however, remains in striking the right balance between innovation and privacy. As the company continues to expand its reach in healthcare and other industries, these ethical questions will become even more pressing. Karp's leadership will play a critical role in navigating these challenges and ensuring that Palantir's technology continues to be used responsibly.

Surveillance and Accountability: The Price of Success

One of the most significant ethical dilemmas Palantir has faced has been the growing perception of its role in enabling surveillance. In the early days of the company, Palantir positioned itself as a company that could help intelligence agencies and government organizations sift through vast amounts of data to find meaningful insights. But as the company grew, so did the concerns about how its technology was being used.

The idea that Palantir's software could be used for mass surveillance became a point of contention when the company's involvement in various high-profile government projects became public. Palantir's work with U.S. Immigration and Customs Enforcement (ICE), in particular, sparked protests and criticism from human rights activists, who argued that the company's technology was being used to track immigrants and assist in deportation efforts. This controversy ignited a debate about Palantir's ethical responsibility, as the company's technology could potentially be used to harm vulnerable populations.

Karp, however, has consistently defended Palantir's work, insisting that the company is committed to human rights and ensuring that its technology is used responsibly. He has argued that Palantir's software is merely a tool and that it is up to the organizations using it to ensure that it is being used ethically. Despite these assertions, Palantir's association with controversial government projects has raised questions about the company's accountability and its role in enabling surveillance.

In response to these concerns, Karp has called for greater transparency in the use of technology, especially in sensitive areas like immigration and law enforcement. He has acknowledged that Palantir must do more to ensure that its technology is not used in ways that infringe on civil liberties, but he has also stressed the importance of safeguarding national security and ensuring that technology is used for the greater good.

Karp's Ethical Leadership: A Vision for Responsible Technology

Despite the controversies and ethical dilemmas that have surrounded Palantir, Alex Karp's leadership has been defined by a commitment to transparency, responsibility, and ethical decision-making. Karp has never shied away from addressing the difficult questions that come with building and deploying powerful technology. He has consistently emphasized that Palantir's mission is to solve critical problems and that ethical considerations must be at the forefront of every decision the company makes.

Karp's approach to leadership has been rooted in the belief that technology, when used responsibly, can be a force for good. He has often spoken about the need for companies like Palantir to be held accountable for the impact of their technology on society, and he has advocated for stronger regulations around data usage, privacy, and surveillance.

Palantir's ethical challenges are far from over. As the company continues to grow and expand into new industries, it will face new questions about how its technology is used and the potential consequences of its deployment. But Karp's leadership provides a framework for navigating these challenges, one that prioritizes responsibility, transparency, and ethical conduct.

Conclusion: Navigating the Ethical Landscape

Palantir's journey has been one marked by ethical dilemmas and controversies, as the company's technology has become increasingly powerful and influential. Under Karp's leadership, the company has worked to navigate these challenges by emphasizing transparency, accountability, and a commitment to responsible data usage. While the company's role in national security, healthcare, and law enforcement continues to raise concerns about privacy and surveillance, Karp has consistently defended Palantir's work and its mission to solve global problems.

The ethical challenges Palantir faces are a reflection of the broader issues facing the tech industry today. As technology becomes more pervasive and powerful, the need for ethical decision-making has never been greater. Karp's leadership will continue to play a pivotal role in ensuring that Palantir's technology is used responsibly and that the company remains accountable for its impact on society.

Chapter 6

Karp's Leadership Philosophy and Vision

In the ever-evolving world of technology, there are certain leaders who not only build successful companies but also redefine how we approach leadership, innovation, and the integration of technology in society. Alex Karp, the co-founder and CEO of Palantir Technologies, is one such leader whose approach to leadership and business has influenced not only the tech industry but also the broader conversations around data, privacy, and ethics in technology. Karp's leadership philosophy is shaped by a combination of intellectual rigor, an unwavering commitment to ethical practices, and a strong belief in the power of technology to solve real-world problems.

In this chapter, we will dive deep into Karp's leadership style, his commitment to transparency, and how his unique perspective on technology, collaboration, and societal impact has made Palantir the influential company it is today. We will explore Karp's approach to running a company, his views on the relationship between government and technology, and his focus on innovation—all while maintaining a keen awareness of the societal and ethical implications of Palantir's work.

A Leader with a Philosophical Foundation

Unlike many tech CEOs, Karp's background is not in engineering or business. Instead, he has a doctorate in social theory, and his academic training has played a significant role in shaping how he leads Palantir. His exposure to philosophical thought, particularly the work of Jürgen Habermas and the Frankfurt School, provided him with a deep understanding of the complexities of human society, governance, and technology's role within it.

Karp's background in social theory influences his leadership philosophy in several key ways. First, he believes that leadership is not just about profit or efficiency, but about understanding the societal impact of a company's work. This perspective is at the heart of Palantir's mission—to use technology to solve real-world problems, while ensuring that its work aligns with the broader values of transparency, privacy, and human rights.

Second, Karp's philosophical background has made him a staunch advocate for the importance of intellectual rigor in decision-making. He approaches business challenges not just from a financial or operational perspective but through a lens that examines the broader ethical and societal implications of every decision. This intellectual foundation is central to his leadership style—

one that emphasizes questioning the status quo, critically evaluating the implications of new technologies, and making decisions that are informed by both data and ethical considerations.

Commitment to Transparency: A Cornerstone of Karp's Leadership

One of the most distinctive features of Alex Karp's leadership style is his commitment to transparency. In an industry that is often criticized for operating behind closed doors, Karp has made transparency a central part of Palantir's ethos. For Karp, transparency is not just a buzzword—it is a fundamental principle that guides how Palantir interacts with its clients, stakeholders, and the public.

Karp's commitment to transparency is evident in Palantir's approach to its technology. Unlike many tech companies that treat their software as proprietary "black boxes," Palantir has emphasized the importance of openness and collaboration. The company's platforms are designed to be interactive and customizable, allowing users to engage directly with data and decision-making processes. This transparency allows Palantir's clients—whether they are government agencies or private companies—to better understand how the software works, how decisions are made, and what assumptions are being built into the data analysis.

Karp's transparency also extends to how Palantir works with government clients. Palantir has faced criticism for its close ties to intelligence agencies and law enforcement, with some questioning the company's role in mass surveillance. Karp has consistently defended Palantir's work, but he has also been open about the ethical dilemmas that come with working in sensitive areas such as national security. He has regularly called for greater transparency in how technology is used by governments, emphasizing the need for oversight, accountability, and public scrutiny.

This commitment to transparency is part of Karp's broader philosophy that technology should not be used in a vacuum. He believes that companies must be open about the tools they build, how they are being used, and the potential impact they may have on society. By championing transparency, Karp hopes to foster a more informed public discourse about the role of technology in governance and society.

The Role of Technology in Society: Karp's Vision for Innovation

At the core of Karp's leadership philosophy is a deep belief in the power of technology to drive positive change. However, Karp is also acutely aware of the challenges that come with this power. In many ways, Karp's leadership is defined by his vision of technology as a tool for societal good—a force that can solve critical problems but must be wielded with caution and responsibility.

Karp's perspective on technology is grounded in the belief that the most important innovations are those that solve real-world problems. Palantir, for instance, was not created to build consumer-facing applications that generate profit through advertising or data collection. Instead, the company was founded to tackle complex issues related to national security, health, and other global challenges. Karp has always emphasized that Palantir's mission is not just about technological innovation for its own sake, but about using that innovation to address issues that matter to society.

One of Karp's most significant contributions has been his focus on how data can be used to solve global challenges. In an era where data is more abundant than ever before, the challenge is no longer in gathering information, but in making sense of it.

Palantir's technology has helped governments and organizations make more informed decisions by providing them with the tools to analyze vast amounts of data, uncover hidden patterns, and make data-driven predictions. Whether it is used to prevent terrorist attacks, optimize healthcare delivery, or detect financial fraud, Palantir's technology has been at the forefront of transforming how organizations leverage data for decision-making.

Karp's vision for the future of technology is not solely focused on efficiency and productivity. He believes that the true power of technology lies in its ability to create a more equitable and just society. Technology, for Karp, should be used to address issues of social inequality, improve public health outcomes, and make governance more transparent and accountable. He sees technology as a means of amplifying human potential, not as a force that replaces or diminishes it.

Collaboration Between Government and Private Sector: A Unique Approach

One of the most unique aspects of Karp's leadership is his approach to the collaboration between government and the private sector. In a world where the relationship between these two sectors is often characterized by mistrust and conflict, Karp has sought to build a bridge between them. He believes that the private sector can bring the innovation and agility needed to solve the complex problems faced by governments, while the government can provide the oversight and regulatory frameworks necessary to ensure that technology is used responsibly.

Palantir's work with government agencies, particularly in national security and law enforcement, has been a point of controversy. Some critics argue that private companies should not be involved in the sensitive work of intelligence and surveillance. Karp, however, has defended Palantir's role, arguing that the company provides a critical service by helping governments analyze data in ways that are transparent, accountable, and respectful of privacy. He has consistently stressed that Palantir's technology is not designed for mass surveillance, but rather to help governments identify patterns, predict risks, and make better decisions.

Karp's approach to collaboration extends beyond government work. He has always sought to build partnerships with organizations across industries, from healthcare to finance to energy. For Karp, collaboration is about bringing together diverse perspectives and expertise to solve problems that no single organization or sector could address on its own. He believes that the most impactful solutions come from cross-sector collaboration, where innovation from the private sector meets the resources and regulatory support of the public sector.

Leadership in Times of Crisis: The COVID-19 Response

Karp's leadership was put to the test during the COVID-19 pandemic. As the world grappled with the health crisis, Palantir's technology became an essential tool for governments and organizations trying to manage the crisis. Palantir helped track the spread of the virus, predict healthcare system demands, and coordinate vaccine distribution. The company's data analytics platforms enabled real-time decision-making that was critical in addressing the rapidly evolving situation.

Karp's leadership during the pandemic reflected his broader approach to technology—one that prioritizes solving urgent problems and addressing the needs of society. He understood that Palantir's technology had the potential to make a significant difference in the global response to the pandemic, and he was committed to ensuring that the company's software was used responsibly to help mitigate the crisis.

The pandemic also highlighted Karp's belief in the importance of transparency. Throughout the crisis, Karp emphasized the need for clear, open communication about the use of technology and data. He advocated for transparency in how governments were using data to manage the crisis and ensure that citizens were informed and empowered to make decisions based on reliable, accurate information.

Conclusion: Karp's Enduring Vision and Leadership Legacy

Alex Karp's leadership style is defined by a commitment to transparency, responsibility, and the ethical use of technology. His background in social theory has shaped his view of technology as a tool for societal good—a force that can solve real-world problems but must be handled with care and consideration. Karp's unique approach to leadership has set Palantir apart in the tech world, where many companies are driven by profit motives alone. Instead, Karp's focus on collaboration, transparency, and the responsible use of technology has allowed Palantir to become a critical player in addressing global challenges.

As Palantir continues to grow and evolve, Karp's leadership will remain at the heart of the company's mission. His vision for the future of technology—one that prioritizes ethics, innovation, and social impact—will continue to shape the company's direction and influence the broader tech industry for years to come. Alex Karp's leadership is not just about running a successful business; it is about using technology to create a better, more just world.

Alex Karp

Chapter 7

The Technological Landscape Under Karp's Influence

In a world where technology has become deeply embedded in every facet of life, few individuals have had as significant an influence on the broader technological landscape as Alex Karp. As the CEO and co-founder of Palantir Technologies, Karp has played a pivotal role in shaping the way industries—from defense and national security to finance and healthcare—use and think about data. Through his leadership, Palantir has become a leader in the field of data analytics, offering powerful tools to organizations seeking to solve some of the world's most complex and pressing problems.

But Karp's influence extends far beyond the success of Palantir. His unique perspective on the role of technology in society, the responsibilities of big tech companies, and the relationship between technology, governance, and ethics has shaped not only how Palantir operates but also how the tech industry at large approaches data, privacy, and responsibility. In this chapter, we will explore Karp's broader influence on the technological landscape, his views on the role of big tech, and how Palantir continues to impact a variety of industries.

Karp's Views on Big Tech and Its Role in Society

One of the defining characteristics of Alex Karp's leadership is his critical stance on the role of big tech in society. While many tech leaders are focused on growth and profitability, Karp has always approached his work with a strong ethical framework. His background in social theory and philosophy has made him deeply reflective about the impact of technology on society. He does not shy away from acknowledging the power and influence of the technology sector, but he also emphasizes the potential dangers of unchecked growth and the concentration of power within a few tech giants.

Karp has long been an advocate for greater regulation and oversight of the tech industry. In several interviews and public statements, he has expressed concern about the immense control that large tech companies like Google, Facebook, and Amazon have over users' data and privacy. For Karp, this concentration of power is not just a business issue—it's a societal issue. He believes that tech companies must be held accountable for the way they use data, especially given the immense impact that data-driven decisions have on everything from political elections to personal privacy.

Karp's views on big tech are informed by his belief in the importance of maintaining a balance between innovation and responsibility. He has been vocal about the need for a robust regulatory framework that ensures that technology serves the public good, rather than solely the interests of a few powerful corporations. Unlike many tech CEOs who have championed deregulation as a way to fuel innovation, Karp has argued that responsible governance is necessary to prevent the misuse of technology, particularly when it comes to sensitive areas like data privacy, surveillance, and national security.

At the same time, Karp has recognized the immense potential that technology has to improve lives and solve critical problems. He is not anti-tech; rather, he is a proponent of technology that is used ethically and transparently. His leadership at Palantir reflects this balanced view—while Palantir has grown into one of the leading companies in the data analytics space, Karp has consistently ensured that the company operates with a strong ethical framework that prioritizes transparency, security, and privacy.

Palantir's Impact on National Security and Defense

One of the most significant areas where Palantir has made a mark is in national security and defense. From its inception, Palantir's primary focus has been to develop powerful tools that help government agencies and military organizations make sense of vast amounts of data. In the wake of the September 11 attacks, the need for more advanced data analytics in the intelligence community became clear, and Palantir's technology was designed to fill this gap.

Karp's vision for Palantir in the defense sector was to create a platform that could integrate multiple data sources—ranging from communications intercepts to financial transactions—and help analysts identify hidden patterns and connections that could provide critical intelligence. Unlike traditional intelligence systems, which were often siloed and inefficient, Palantir's software allowed analysts to work collaboratively and dynamically, quickly drawing insights from diverse datasets.

One of Palantir's key innovations was its ability to link together vast amounts of unstructured data—data that didn't fit neatly into traditional databases or systems. By allowing intelligence agencies to visualize connections between seemingly unrelated pieces of information, Palantir's technology helped uncover terrorist networks, disrupt criminal organizations, and prevent future attacks. In this way, Palantir revolutionized the way governments and defense agencies approached data analytics, making it possible to process and analyze large-scale datasets in real-time.

However, Palantir's role in national security has not been without controversy. The company's close ties to government agencies, particularly in the areas of surveillance and counterterrorism, have sparked debates about the potential for abuse. Critics have raised concerns that Palantir's software could be used for mass surveillance or to infringe on civil liberties, particularly in areas like immigration and law enforcement. These concerns have led to protests and calls for greater scrutiny of Palantir's work.

Karp has responded to these concerns by emphasizing the importance of transparency and ethical oversight in Palantir's work with government agencies. He has consistently argued that Palantir's technology is not designed for mass surveillance, but rather for specific, targeted efforts to prevent harm and protect national security. He has also called for greater accountability in the use of technology by governments, stressing that technology should be used responsibly and in a way that respects individual rights.

Transforming the Financial Sector: Palantir's Role in Risk Management and Fraud Prevention

Beyond national security, Palantir has also made significant strides in transforming the financial sector. The company's data analytics platforms have been used by financial institutions to detect fraudulent activities, manage risk, and optimize trading strategies. As the financial industry has become increasingly data-driven, Palantir's technology has provided banks and investment firms with powerful tools to analyze vast amounts of financial data and identify patterns that could indicate fraudulent behavior.

In particular, Palantir's software has been used to track suspicious transactions, identify money laundering activities, and prevent financial crimes before they escalate. By analyzing data across different systems, Palantir's technology can flag irregularities that may not be immediately apparent to human analysts. This predictive capability has allowed financial institutions to reduce their exposure to risk and improve their overall security posture.

Palantir's work in finance has also extended to areas like market analysis and optimization. By leveraging big data and machine learning, Palantir's platforms help financial institutions understand market trends, identify investment opportunities, and optimize their operations. Palantir's ability to process vast amounts of data and provide actionable insights has made it a valuable tool in a sector where every decision can have significant financial consequences.

Despite the success of Palantir's financial sector offerings, the company's role in the industry has raised questions about the ethics of using such powerful technology in a profit-driven environment. Critics argue that the financial industry already wields significant power over global economies, and the use of advanced data analytics only exacerbates this power imbalance. However, Karp has consistently defended Palantir's work, emphasizing that the company's technology is used to improve transparency, reduce fraud, and ensure fairness in financial markets.

Palantir's Healthcare Revolution: Improving Patient Outcomes and System Efficiency

Another sector where Palantir's impact has been profound is healthcare. The healthcare industry is awash in data—patient records, clinical trials, medical research, and health trends—but much of this data remains fragmented and siloed, making it difficult for organizations to make informed decisions. Palantir's technology has been instrumental in helping healthcare providers make sense of this data, providing them with the tools to improve patient outcomes, optimize resources, and streamline operations.

Palantir's work in healthcare includes projects that help hospitals track patient data across various systems, monitor patient progress, and identify potential health risks. By integrating data from multiple sources, Palantir enables healthcare organizations to gain a comprehensive view of a patient's health, allowing for more personalized and effective treatment plans.

The company's software has also been used to help address public health challenges, such as the COVID-19 pandemic. Palantir's technology played a critical role in helping governments and health organizations track the spread of the virus, allocate resources effectively, and predict future healthcare needs. By analyzing trends and data from across the globe, Palantir's platform helped organizations make data-driven decisions that were crucial in responding to the pandemic.

Palantir's influence in healthcare also extends to the realm of medical research. By enabling researchers to analyze vast datasets and uncover new insights, Palantir has played a key role in accelerating medical research and improving clinical outcomes. However, like in other industries, Palantir's involvement in healthcare has raised concerns about privacy and the ethical use of patient data. Karp has consistently emphasized that Palantir's technology is used to improve healthcare delivery and patient outcomes, while adhering to strict ethical standards for data privacy and security.

Karp's Legacy and the Future of Technology

As we look to the future, it is clear that Karp's influence on the technological landscape will continue to shape industries and impact society. His commitment to responsible technology, his focus on data privacy, and his belief in the power of innovation to solve global challenges have set a new standard for leadership in the tech world. Palantir's work in national security, finance, healthcare, and beyond has already transformed these industries, and the company's continued growth will likely lead to even more significant innovations.

Karp's leadership philosophy—a combination of intellectual rigor, ethical responsibility, and a commitment to using technology for the greater good—has made him one of the most influential figures in the tech industry. As technology continues to evolve, Karp's influence will remain a guiding force, ensuring that innovation is used responsibly and for the benefit of society as a whole.

Conclusion

Under Alex Karp's leadership, Palantir Technologies has become a transformative force in the world of data analytics, helping organizations across a range of industries solve complex problems and make informed, data-driven decisions. Karp's unique perspective on the role of technology in society—his belief in transparency, accountability, and the ethical use of data— has shaped not only Palantir's operations but the broader technological landscape. Whether in national security, finance, healthcare, or beyond, Palantir continues to impact industries around the world, driving innovation while navigating the complex ethical and societal issues that arise from the power of technology. Karp's legacy will undoubtedly continue to shape the future of technology for years to come.

Chapter 8

A Look Toward the Future

The future of technology is both exciting and uncertain, shaped by the rapid pace of innovation and the increasing influence of artificial intelligence (AI), machine learning, and data analytics on every aspect of society. Alex Karp, as the co-founder and CEO of Palantir Technologies, has been at the forefront of this technological revolution. His leadership and vision have helped shape Palantir into a company that uses data to solve some of the world's most complex problems, ranging from national security to healthcare. But Karp's influence extends far beyond Palantir's success; it's embedded in his broader vision for the future of technology, including the pivotal role of AI and machine learning in solving humanity's most pressing challenges.

This chapter reflects on Karp's vision for the future of technology, examining his thoughts on AI, machine learning, data analytics, and the ethical responsibilities of tech companies. As the world stands on the brink of new technological frontiers, Karp's insights provide a window into what the future holds—and the role that technology will play in shaping society, governance, and global challenges.

A Vision for Artificial Intelligence: Beyond Automation to Problem Solving

Artificial intelligence (AI) and machine learning are at the heart of much of Karp's vision for the future. While many tech leaders focus on AI as a tool for automation and efficiency, Karp's approach is more expansive. For Karp, AI isn't just about replacing human labor or speeding up processes. It's about using technology to solve some of the world's most complex and intractable problems, ones that have stymied humanity for centuries. From combating climate change to predicting health outcomes to identifying emerging threats to global security, Karp sees AI as a tool that can empower people to make better, more informed decisions.

Karp believes that AI, when applied thoughtfully and responsibly, can amplify human capabilities and expand the scope of what is possible in solving large-scale issues. But AI is not a panacea. It requires careful consideration, ethical guidelines, and constant oversight to ensure that its potential is harnessed for good. Karp has been vocal about his concerns that, in the rush to develop and deploy AI, many companies and governments are not giving enough thought to its long-term implications. The use of AI in decision-making must not only be accurate but also transparent, accountable, and aligned with the values of the societies that it serves.

For Karp, the future of AI should focus on creating systems that help people—whether through better healthcare, more efficient energy use, or more secure societies—while keeping ethics at the forefront. AI will not just enhance productivity; it will empower humans to tackle challenges that are currently beyond our capabilities. The key is ensuring that AI serves humanity and is designed in a way that respects the ethical boundaries and considerations that are essential for a just society.

Machine Learning: A Path to Predictive Power

Alongside AI, machine learning (ML) is another central aspect of Karp's future vision. While AI encompasses a broad range of technologies, machine learning is a specific subset of AI that focuses on training algorithms to learn from data and make predictions or decisions based on that data.

Machine learning, in essence, allows systems to "learn" without being explicitly programmed for every task. This ability is at the core of Palantir's data analytics platforms, which can process vast amounts of information to uncover hidden patterns and make informed predictions.

Karp sees machine learning as an essential tool for not just analyzing past data but also predicting future trends. In sectors like healthcare, finance, and national security, machine learning offers the ability to anticipate risks and outcomes before they happen. By analyzing historical data, machine learning algorithms can help organizations predict which patients are at risk for certain conditions, which financial transactions might indicate fraud, or where security threats might emerge.

One of the most compelling aspects of machine learning, according to Karp, is its potential to revolutionize problem-solving in areas where traditional methods fall short. Machine learning can sift through vast amounts of data—data that would be impossible for humans to analyze in real-time—and uncover patterns that are not immediately obvious. This predictive power is a game-changer for industries that rely on data-driven decision-making, and Karp believes that as machine learning continues to evolve, its applications will expand exponentially.

However, Karp is quick to point out that machine learning also comes with its own set of ethical concerns. The algorithms that drive machine learning are only as good as the data they are trained on, and biased or incomplete data can lead to inaccurate or discriminatory outcomes. Karp has emphasized the need for oversight and accountability in machine learning, particularly in sectors like law enforcement and healthcare, where biased algorithms can have serious consequences for individuals' lives. He believes that we must be vigilant in ensuring that machine learning is used responsibly and that its potential is fully realized without compromising fairness or justice.

Data's Role in Solving Global Challenges

One of Karp's most compelling beliefs is that data is not just an asset—it is a powerful tool that can be used to solve the world's most pressing issues. From climate change to public health to poverty, data has the potential to drive solutions that can have a transformative impact on society. In Karp's vision, data is not just about collecting information; it's about using that information to make better, more informed decisions that benefit society as a whole.

Palantir has already demonstrated how data analytics can drive meaningful change in fields like national security and healthcare. But Karp's vision for the future extends far beyond these areas. He believes that data analytics can play a key role in tackling climate change, for example, by enabling governments and businesses to track environmental trends, optimize energy usage, and predict the long-term effects of climate policies. By integrating data from various sources—from environmental sensors to satellite imagery—Palantir's technology can help organizations understand the complex dynamics of the natural world and make decisions that mitigate the impact of climate change.

In addition to environmental challenges, Karp sees data as a critical tool for addressing public health crises. As seen with the COVID-19 pandemic, the ability to collect and analyze health data in real-time is crucial for managing global health emergencies. Data-driven decision-making can help governments predict the spread of diseases, allocate resources efficiently, and track vaccination efforts. But beyond crisis management, Karp believes that data analytics can help revolutionize healthcare by identifying patterns in patient data, optimizing treatment plans, and improving outcomes for individuals.

For Karp, the future of data is about harnessing its power to address systemic problems—problems that are too complex and multifaceted for any one organization or individual to solve alone. By breaking down silos and enabling better collaboration across industries, data can drive solutions that improve lives, safeguard the environment, and create more equitable societies.

Collaboration Between Tech and Government: A Key to the Future

One of the central themes of Karp's vision for the future is the need for greater collaboration between the tech industry and governments. In recent years, there has been a growing tension between the private sector and government regulators, particularly in areas like data privacy, cybersecurity, and surveillance. While many tech companies have grown to dominate global markets, Karp believes that the most pressing challenges of the future—whether in national security, public health, or the environment—cannot be solved by the private sector alone.

For Karp, the future of technology requires collaboration between tech companies, governments, and civil society. Governments provide the regulatory frameworks that ensure technology is used responsibly, while the private sector brings innovation, expertise, and agility to the table. In Karp's view, the best solutions come from partnerships where both sides bring their strengths to bear on the most critical challenges of the future.

This philosophy is reflected in Palantir's work with government agencies around the world. Palantir's technology has been instrumental in helping governments solve complex problems, but Karp has always emphasized that this work must be done with transparency, oversight, and respect for civil liberties. He has repeatedly called for stronger collaboration between the public and private sectors to ensure that technology is used for the greater good, rather than for profit-driven motives.

The Ethical Challenges of the Future

As the future of technology unfolds, one of the biggest challenges Karp anticipates is the ethical dilemmas that will arise from the continued expansion of AI, machine learning, and data analytics. While these technologies have immense potential to solve complex problems, they also present significant risks, particularly in areas like privacy, bias, and accountability.

Karp has consistently advocated for greater ethical oversight of technology. He believes that tech companies, especially those working with sensitive data, must be held accountable for how their products are used and the impact they have on society. As AI and machine learning continue to evolve, Karp stresses the importance of developing ethical frameworks that prioritize fairness, transparency, and accountability.

For Karp, the future of technology isn't just about innovation—it's about ensuring that technology serves humanity, rather than the other way around. He believes that technology should be developed with a sense of responsibility, ensuring that its benefits are distributed equitably and that its risks are mitigated through careful oversight.

Conclusion: A Future Shaped by Responsibility and Innovation

As we look toward the future of technology, it is clear that Alex Karp's vision will continue to shape the way we think about and use technology in the coming decades. His focus on responsible innovation, ethical oversight, and the power of data to solve global challenges provides a roadmap for how we can navigate the complexities of the digital age.

Karp's leadership has demonstrated that technology can be a force for good, but only if it is developed and used with care, responsibility, and a strong commitment to ethical principles. Whether in AI, machine learning, data analytics, or other emerging technologies, Karp's vision for the future reminds us that technology must always serve humanity—not the other way around.

As Palantir continues to innovate and grow, Karp's influence will remain a guiding force in shaping the future of technology. His vision for a more collaborative, transparent, and ethically-driven tech industry will help ensure that technology continues to drive progress while safeguarding the values that make society stronger. The future is bright, but it must be one where technology serves a higher purpose—a purpose that benefits us all.

Conclusion

A Legacy of Innovation and Impact

Alex Karp's journey as a tech leader is a testament to the power of vision, innovation, and ethical responsibility. His work has not only reshaped the world of data analytics but has also influenced the broader technological landscape in ways that continue to resonate across industries and generations. Karp's contributions have left a lasting impact on technology and society, demonstrating that technological progress is not solely about advancing systems or creating new products—it is about leveraging innovation to solve complex, global challenges in a way that is responsible, transparent, and beneficial to all.

As we reflect on Karp's legacy, it becomes clear that his influence goes far beyond the success of Palantir Technologies. While Palantir has undeniably revolutionized industries ranging from national security to healthcare, Karp's broader impact lies in his philosophical approach to leadership, technology, and ethics. This final chapter explores the enduring influence of Alex Karp's work, how it continues to inspire innovation, shape industries, and set the stage for the next generation of tech leaders.

The Birth of a Tech Giant: Palantir's Impact on Industry

When Alex Karp co-founded Palantir Technologies in 2003, the vision for the company was clear: to harness the power of data analytics to solve some of the world's most complex problems. In the early 2000s, the world was beginning to realize that the vast amount of data generated daily could be a powerful tool for solving problems across a range of sectors—from government and national security to healthcare and finance. But with this power came responsibility. The challenge was not just building the technology, but ensuring it was used ethically and transparently.

Karp's leadership and vision for Palantir have transformed the company into one of the most influential players in the world of data analytics. The company's software has been instrumental in helping intelligence agencies prevent terrorist attacks, tracking fraud in the financial sector, and optimizing healthcare delivery. By providing powerful, scalable tools for integrating and analyzing data, Palantir has revolutionized industries that rely on large, complex datasets—industries where traditional methods of data analysis were often inadequate.

However, Palantir's true legacy lies in the way it has demonstrated the value of data analytics in solving real-world problems.

Through its work with governments and private sector clients, Palantir has shown that data is not just a commodity to be exploited for profit, but a resource that can be used to address pressing societal challenges. Karp's leadership and commitment to using data for good have influenced how other tech companies and industries approach the role of data in their operations.

Karp's Vision for Ethical Innovation: A Model for Tech Leadership

Karp's leadership style has been shaped by a strong ethical framework that emphasizes transparency, responsibility, and the role of technology in serving society. Unlike many leaders in Silicon Valley who prioritize growth and profit above all else, Karp has always maintained that technology should be developed with careful consideration of its impact on society. He has advocated for greater regulation and oversight of the tech industry, stressing that companies must be held accountable for how they use data and the consequences of their technological innovations.

His approach to leadership is rooted in his academic background in social theory. Karp's understanding of human society, governance, and ethics has influenced how he runs Palantir and how the company engages with its clients. He has consistently emphasized that Palantir's technology must be used to solve critical problems, rather than being deployed for profit-driven motives or for the sake of technological advancement alone. This emphasis on ethics and responsibility has set Karp apart from many other tech leaders and has been a key factor in Palantir's success.

Karp's commitment to transparency and ethical leadership has also influenced other companies in the tech industry. In a time when issues of data privacy, surveillance, and security are at the forefront of public discourse, Karp has shown that it is possible to build a successful tech company while maintaining high standards of accountability. His leadership has demonstrated that tech companies can thrive without compromising their ethical obligations to society.

Inspiring Innovation Across Industries

Beyond Palantir's direct impact on industries like national security and healthcare, Karp's work has inspired a broader shift in how companies approach innovation. As more industries begin to embrace data analytics, AI, and machine learning, Karp's approach to technology—one that balances innovation with responsibility—provides a model for future tech leaders.

One of the most significant ways in which Karp has inspired innovation is by showing that technology does not have to be siloed into separate industries. Palantir's cross-industry success, particularly its ability to serve clients in both government and the private sector, has set an example for other companies looking to scale their technology across different domains. By demonstrating the power of data analytics in addressing a wide range of problems—from healthcare optimization to fraud detection in financial markets—Karp has shown that the future of technology lies in creating versatile, adaptable solutions that can be applied across industries.

Moreover, Karp's focus on collaboration between sectors has had a profound impact on how businesses think about the relationship between tech and government. Where many tech companies see government work as a niche or a regulatory hurdle, Karp has emphasized the importance of partnerships between the public and private sectors. For Karp, the most pressing challenges—whether in healthcare, security, or climate change—cannot be solved by any one entity alone. Instead, it requires a collaborative approach where both sectors bring their strengths to the table. This vision has influenced how tech companies work with governments, leading to more open and transparent collaborations in tackling global issues.

Karp's Influence on the Next Generation of Tech Leaders

As technology continues to shape the world in profound ways, Karp's leadership provides a blueprint for the next generation of tech innovators. His commitment to ethical innovation, transparency, and the responsible use of data has set a high standard for future tech leaders. Karp's example shows that it is possible to build a successful tech company while maintaining a strong moral compass and addressing society's most pressing challenges.

In an era where the power of tech companies often extends beyond the reach of regulation, Karp's leadership provides a refreshing reminder that technology can—and should— be used for the greater good. His belief that tech companies have a responsibility to society has influenced not only Palantir's internal practices but also the broader conversation about the role of technology in modern governance and society.

By advocating for greater oversight, regulation, and transparency, Karp has helped shift the conversation in Silicon Valley and beyond. He has shown that tech leaders can take a more active role in shaping public policy and ensuring that their innovations benefit society as a whole, rather than just their shareholders. His legacy is one of leadership that prioritizes long-term societal impact over short-term profits—a model that is sure to inspire future generations of tech entrepreneurs.

Shaping the Future of Data and Technology

Karp's legacy also lies in his vision for the future of data and technology. As data continues to grow exponentially and new technologies like AI and machine learning transform the way we live and work, Karp's work has laid the groundwork for how these technologies can be used to solve complex problems. His insistence on using data for good, coupled with his focus on ethical considerations, has set a precedent for how future technologies should be developed and deployed.

Palantir's continued success in areas like defense, healthcare, and finance is a testament to the power of data-driven decision-making. But Karp's vision extends beyond these industries. As the world faces challenges like climate change, social inequality, and global health crises, Karp's belief that data and technology can provide solutions remains a guiding principle for how we should approach these issues. In the years to come, his influence will continue to shape how technology is used to tackle some of the world's most pressing problems, ensuring that innovation serves the needs of society rather than undermining its values.

Karp's Lasting Impact: A Legacy Built on Responsibility

Ultimately, Alex Karp's legacy is built on his commitment to responsibility and ethical leadership. While many tech companies have focused on maximizing profits, Karp's vision for Palantir has always been about using technology to make a difference in the world. His belief in the power of data to solve global challenges, paired with his focus on transparency, privacy, and accountability, has set Palantir apart as a company that values more than just financial success.

As Karp steps into the future, his influence will continue to resonate across the tech industry and beyond. His contributions to the world of data analytics, AI, and machine learning will shape the direction of technology for years to come, providing a roadmap for future leaders who will carry the torch of innovation, responsibility, and societal impact.

Karp's legacy is one of enduring innovation and ethical leadership, and his influence will continue to inspire generations of tech leaders who are committed to using technology for the greater good. As the world faces ever more complex challenges, Karp's vision reminds us that technology can—and should—be a force for positive change, one that serves society, not just profits.

Appendices

A: Timeline of Key Milestones in Alex Karp's Career

Alex Karp's career has been marked by groundbreaking achievements, both in the tech industry and in shaping the way technology impacts global challenges. Below is a timeline of key milestones in his career, highlighting the pivotal moments that have defined his path as a visionary leader in the tech world.

1967: Alex Karp is born in Philadelphia, Pennsylvania. Raised in a family that values education, Karp's early years are marked by a deep curiosity and an interest in philosophy and social theory.

1989-1994: Karp attends the University of Chicago, where he studies history and social theory, an academic background that would later shape his leadership and philosophy in the tech world.

1994-1998: Karp pursues a doctorate in social theory at Goethe University in Frankfurt, Germany, studying under renowned philosopher Jürgen Habermas. His academic work influences his later views on governance, technology, and social responsibility.

2003: Alex Karp co-founds Palantir Technologies in Silicon Valley with Peter Thiel and several other entrepreneurs. The company is built with the vision of revolutionizing data analytics for governments, businesses, and organizations by providing advanced tools to integrate and analyze large datasets.

2004: Palantir receives early investment from Thiel and others, enabling the company to begin working on its flagship products, Palantir Foundry and Palantir Gotham, both designed to help organizations analyze large datasets and uncover hidden insights.

2004-2006: Palantir secures early contracts with U.S. government agencies, particularly in national security. The company's software is used to help prevent terrorism by analyzing intelligence data in real-time, a breakthrough that solidifies Palantir's role in the defense and intelligence sectors.

2008: Karp takes the helm as CEO of Palantir, a role that would define his leadership and vision for the company. Under his guidance, Palantir begins to expand its reach beyond government clients and into the private sector.

2010: Palantir enters the private sector, expanding its client base to include financial institutions, healthcare organizations, and corporate clients. The company's software is used to track fraud, optimize operations, and solve other complex business problems.

2013: Palantir's work with government agencies such as the U.S. Department of Defense, FBI, and CIA continues to gain attention. However, this also leads to criticism and protests over privacy concerns, especially regarding the company's role in surveillance.

2015-2016: Palantir plays a critical role in healthcare, particularly in public health efforts such as tracking and managing diseases, as well as optimizing hospital operations and patient care. Palantir's work with healthcare organizations expands significantly.

2017: Palantir partners with several international governments to help them address complex global challenges, including counterterrorism and public health issues. The company also begins exploring new applications for its technology in sectors such as energy and manufacturing.

2019: Palantir goes public through a direct listing on the New York Stock Exchange, marking a major milestone in the company's history. The move allows the company to further expand its global presence while continuing its work in data analytics and AI-driven problem-solving.

2021: Under Karp's leadership, Palantir continues to innovate in the fields of AI and machine learning, partnering with governments and businesses to tackle a wide range of challenges, including COVID-19 response, cybersecurity, and climate change.

Present Day: Alex Karp remains at the helm of Palantir, continuing to shape the future of technology and data analytics. He is a thought leader in the tech industry, advocating for responsible technology use, transparency, and ethical oversight.

B: Palantir's Major Projects and Achievements

Palantir Technologies has played a central role in transforming how organizations use data to make decisions and solve complex problems. Below is a summary of some of Palantir's most significant projects and achievements, illustrating the company's far-reaching impact across multiple sectors.

1. National Security and Counterterrorism

One of Palantir's most well-known early projects was its work with U.S. intelligence agencies following the September 11 attacks. The company's software was designed to help agencies like the CIA, FBI, and Department of Defense analyze vast amounts of intelligence data, connecting disparate pieces of information to uncover terrorist plots and prevent attacks.

Preventing Terrorist Attacks: Palantir's technology helped agencies make critical connections between pieces of intelligence, enabling them to track down terrorist cells and thwart potential attacks.

Tracking Global Terror Networks: Palantir's tools were instrumental in helping intelligence agencies track the movement and communication of terrorist groups across borders, ultimately aiding in dismantling global terrorist networks.

2. Financial Sector and Fraud Detection

Palantir's technology revolutionized how financial institutions approached fraud detection and risk management. By integrating multiple datasets, Palantir's software enabled banks and financial organizations to uncover fraudulent transactions, identify suspicious patterns, and manage risk more effectively.

Fraud Prevention: Palantir worked with major financial institutions to detect anomalies in financial transactions, preventing millions of dollars in potential fraud.

Compliance and Regulation: Palantir's technology has been used to help financial institutions comply with regulatory requirements by providing the ability to analyze and report complex data.

3. Healthcare and Public Health

Healthcare has become one of the most significant sectors where Palantir has made an impact. The company has worked with healthcare organizations, government health agencies, and research institutions to optimize healthcare delivery, improve patient outcomes, and track disease outbreaks.

Managing COVID-19 Response: During the COVID-19 pandemic, Palantir's software was used to track the spread of the virus, manage vaccine distribution, and allocate resources to hospitals and healthcare providers in real-time.

Optimizing Healthcare Operations: Palantir has partnered with healthcare organizations to integrate and analyze patient data across various platforms, improving diagnosis, treatment, and hospital efficiency.

4. Humanitarian Aid and Disaster Relief

Palantir has also been involved in humanitarian and disaster relief efforts, using its technology to assist in crisis response and resource allocation.

Hurricane Relief Efforts: In the aftermath of natural disasters like Hurricane Katrina and

Hurricane Maria, Palantir's software has been used to coordinate relief efforts, ensuring that resources were directed to the areas of greatest need.

Humanitarian Crises: Palantir's technology has been used in conflict zones to track refugees, assess needs, and manage resources for displaced populations.

5. Energy and Environmental Sustainability

Palantir has extended its work into the energy sector, helping organizations optimize operations, reduce waste, and improve environmental sustainability.

Energy Optimization: Palantir has partnered with energy companies to analyze data from various sources (e.g., sensors, equipment) to improve efficiency, reduce costs, and ensure sustainable energy production.

Climate Change Initiatives: The company's data analytics platforms have been used to track environmental data, model the effects of climate change, and help organizations develop strategies to reduce their carbon footprint.

6. AI and Machine Learning Integration

Palantir continues to integrate artificial intelligence and machine learning into its platforms, helping clients make predictive decisions, automate processes, and gain insights from complex datasets.

AI-Driven Predictions: Palantir's machine learning tools are used by governments and businesses to predict trends, from market shifts in the finance sector to the spread of diseases in healthcare.

Machine Learning for Optimization: In industries like manufacturing and supply chain management, Palantir's AI tools help optimize workflows, reduce inefficiencies, and improve decision-making.

C: Selected Writings and Speeches by Alex Karp

Alex Karp has long been an advocate for responsible technology, transparency, and the ethical use of data. His public speeches and writings have helped shape the broader conversation around the role of technology in modern governance and society. Below is a selection of some of Karp's most impactful writings and speeches, providing insights into his philosophy and vision for the future.

1. "The Dangers of Unchecked Technology"
In this essay, Karp explores the rapid growth of technology and the increasing concentration of power within a few tech companies. He argues for greater regulation and oversight of the tech industry,

emphasizing the need for a responsible approach to data use that prioritizes the public good.

2. "Data as a Tool for Good: A New Approach to Innovation"
In this speech, Karp discusses the transformative potential of data and analytics in solving global challenges. He argues that data, when used ethically, can be a force for good—helping governments, businesses, and individuals make better decisions, solve complex problems, and create positive social impact.

3. "The Ethical Use of AI and Machine Learning"
In this address, Karp dives into the ethical implications of artificial intelligence and machine learning, calling for the responsible development and use of these technologies. He stresses the importance of transparency, accountability, and oversight in ensuring

that AI benefits society while minimizing risks.

4. "The Role of Tech in Modern Governance"
This speech examines the relationship between the tech industry and government. Karp argues for a closer collaboration between the public and private sectors to tackle pressing global issues, such as climate change, cybersecurity, and public health.

5. "Leading with Integrity: Palantir's Commitment to Responsibility"
In this piece, Karp reflects on Palantir's mission and its commitment to ethical innovation. He discusses the importance of maintaining a strong ethical framework in the development and deployment of technology, particularly in sectors like national security and healthcare.

Through his career, Alex Karp has not only built a successful company but also influenced the way technology is viewed and used in society. His contributions continue to shape industries and inspire future generations of tech leaders, all while keeping ethical considerations and responsibility at the core of technological innovation.